D1061176

The Human Body

The Circulatory System

Kristin Petrie MS, RD • ABDO Publishing Company

visit us at
www.abdopublishing.com

Published by ABDO Publishing Company, 4940 Viking Drive, Edina, Minnesota 55435.

Printed in the United States.

Cover Photo: Corbis
Interior Photos: © Articulate Graphics/Custom Medical Stock Photo pp. 7, 26; Corbis pp. 1, 5, 8, 11, 15, 17, 19, 23, 27, 29; © Custom Medical Stock Photo p. 9; © Educational Images/Custom Medical Stock Photo pp. 16, 25; Index Stock p. 12; © L.Birmingham/Custom Medical Stock Photo pp. 21, 24; © L.Morgan/Custom Medical Stock Photo p. 18; © P.Bennis/Custom Medical Stock Photo p. 13; Visuals Unlimited p. 4

Series Coordinator: Heidi M. Dahmes
Editors: Heidi M. Dahmes, Megan M. Gunderson
Art Direction: Neil Klinepier

Library of Congress Cataloging-in-Publication Data

Petrie, Kristin, 1970-
The circulatory system / Kristin Petrie.
p. cm. -- (The human body)
Includes index.
ISBN-10 1-59679-709-6
ISBN-13 978-1-59679-709-3
1. Cardiovascular system--Juvenile literature. I. Title.

QP103.P375 2006
612.1--dc22

2005049311

Contents

Delivery System 4
The Heart 6
Blood 10
Blood Vessels 14
Pit Stop at the Cells 16
The Return Trip 18
The Lungs and the Kidneys 20
A Trip Around the Body 22
Diseases 26
Healthy Upkeep 28
Glossary 30
Saying It 31
Web Sites 31
Index 32

DELIVERY SYSTEM

Does your heart beat faster when you are in a hurry? Have you ever said, "Thanks, lungs!" when you've had to catch your breath? Does blood make you uneasy? Be grateful for these things. Without your heart pumping blood throughout your body, you couldn't survive.

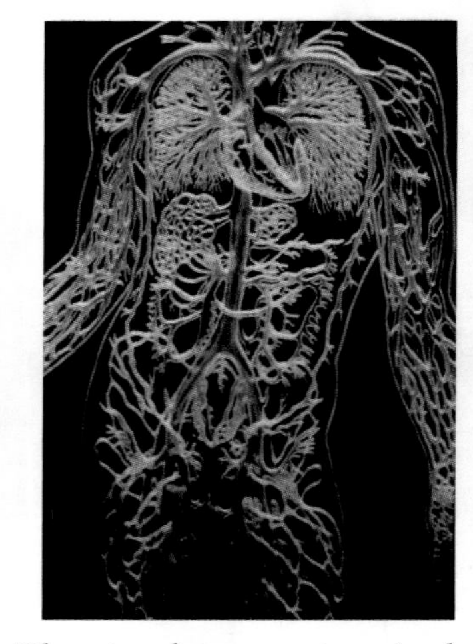

The circulatory system is also called the cardiovascular system. This vital system is in charge of delivering blood to your body's tissues.

The circulatory system consists of the heart, the blood vessels, and the blood that is pumped through them. The circulatory system has many jobs. One of its most important jobs is transporting oxygen and **nutrients** throughout your body. Equally important, it carries away waste products.

Your circulatory system does other jobs, too. It sends out disease fighters. It keeps you at the right temperature on hot and cold days. And, your circulatory system carries its own first aid kit. What would you do without scabs to stop dirt from entering a wound?

Smile! Your circulatory system is working without any thought from you.

The Heart

The heart is the most appreciated part of the circulatory system. This is with good reason. In your lifetime, your heart will beat more than 2 billion times! Leg muscles may tire after a run. And, arm muscles may grow weary after swimming laps. But, your heart's cardiac muscle keeps going.

Your heart sits between your lungs and behind your sternum, or breastbone. The heart is an important **organ** that is about as big as a large, clenched fist. It weighs less than one pound (450 g).

The heart has thick, muscular walls. These walls divide it into four chambers. The two top chambers are called atria. Atria fill with the blood returning to the heart from the body and lungs. When full, the atria contract. This action squeezes the blood into the two lower chambers called ventricles.

Ventricles are larger and more muscular than atria. Their walls are thicker because they have a harder task. They push blood out of the heart and back into blood vessels. The left ventricle is strong enough to push blood all the way to your feet!

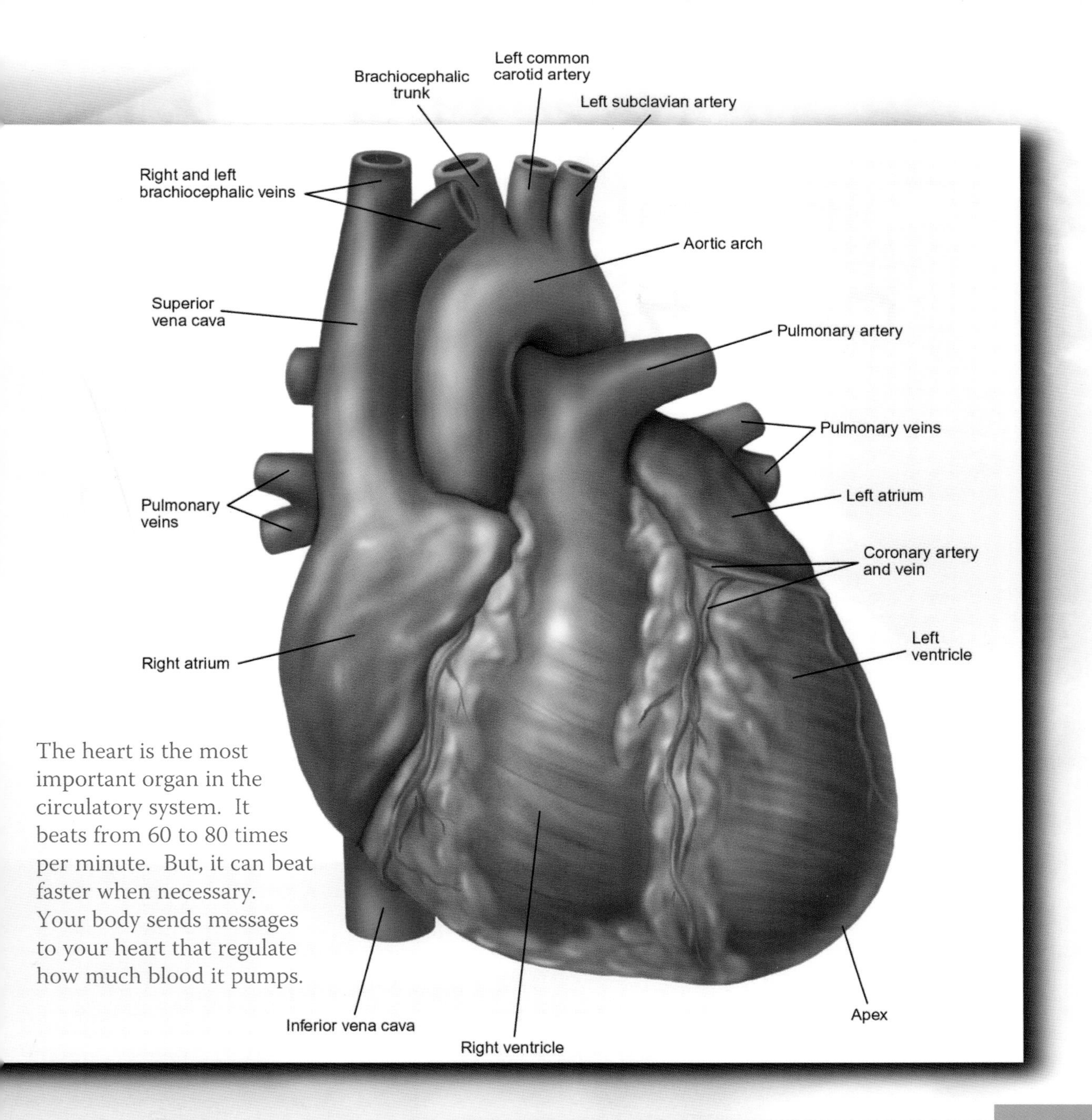

The heart is the most important organ in the circulatory system. It beats from 60 to 80 times per minute. But, it can beat faster when necessary. Your body sends messages to your heart that regulate how much blood it pumps.

The atria and ventricles work together. When the atria are full, a "door" opens and blood rushes into the ventricles. After the ventricles are full, the heart contracts again and another "door" opens. Blood rushes out of the ventricles and into the body. At the same time, the atria are filling again.

Four strong **valves** keep blood moving in the right direction through your heart. The mitral and tricuspid valves are between the atria and the ventricles. The aortic and **pulmonary** valves control blood flow out of the heart. These valves open and close with each heartbeat.

Now, pay attention to your heartbeat. Do you

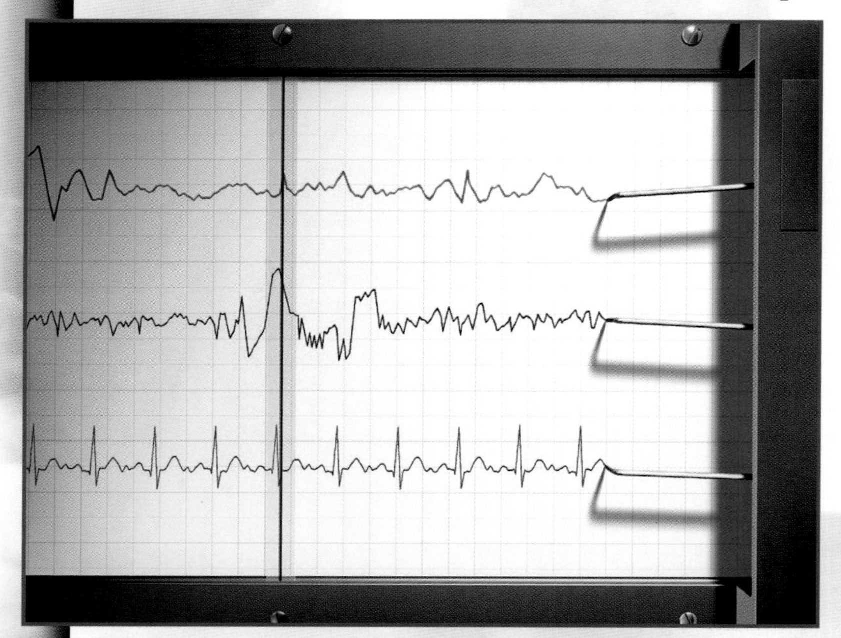

An electrocardiograph measures the electric current produced by the heart muscle during a heartbeat. The readings provide information on the condition and performance of the heart.

hear a "lub-dup" sound? That is your ventricles contracting and sending blood into **pulmonary** and systemic circulation.

Pulmonary circulation carries blood along blood vessels from the heart to the lungs. Systemic circulation carries blood between the heart and all of the other body **tissues**.

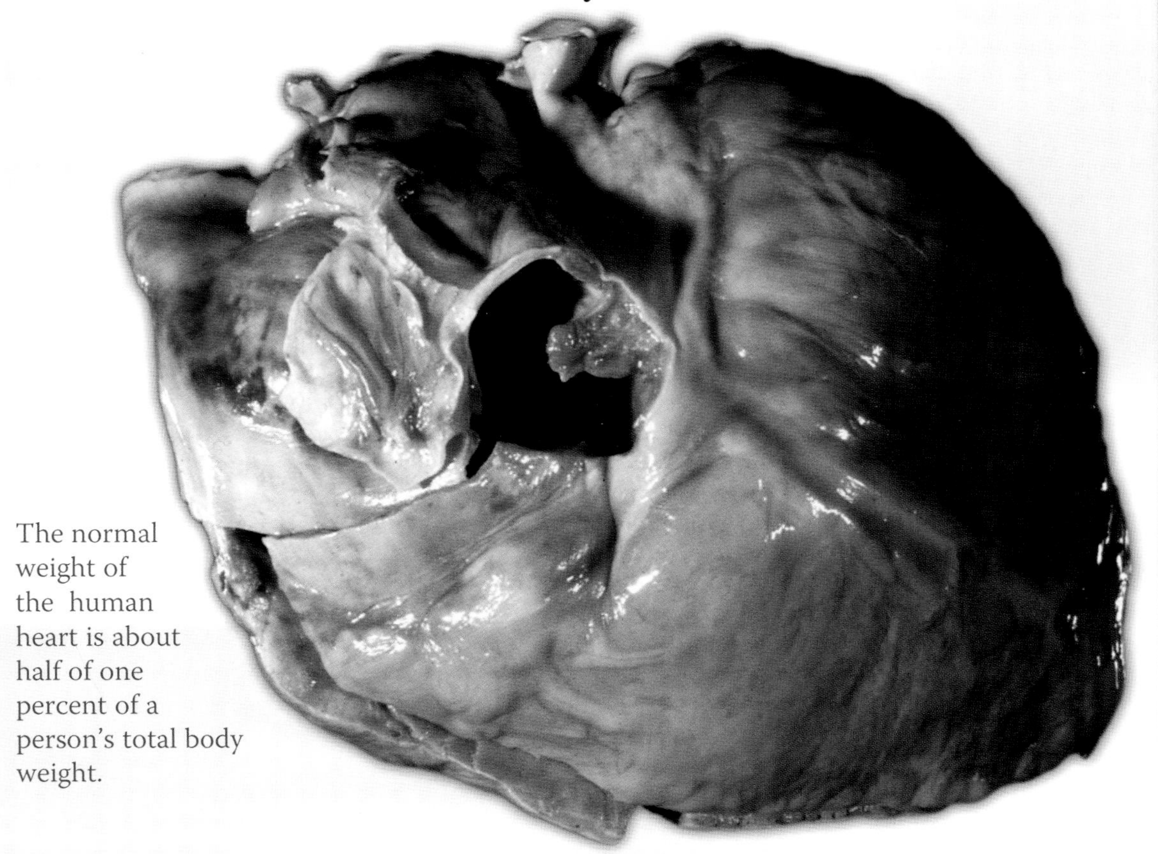

The normal weight of the human heart is about half of one percent of a person's total body weight.

Blood

Even before microscopes and Band-Aids, people knew the importance of blood. Your blood has many critical jobs. It supplies oxygen to your cells and removes their wastes. It also gives food and vitamins to the cells. To get its work done, it must be made of different materials. So, blood is a mixture of cells and plasma.

Plasma is the biggest component of blood. It is a watery, yellowish liquid. There are three kinds of cells in plasma. These are red blood cells, white blood cells, and platelets.

Red blood cells carry oxygen from the lungs to your body's **tissues**. They also take away carbon dioxide to be eliminated from the body. Carbon dioxide is a waste product of your cells. Red blood cells contain the protein hemoglobin. When combined with oxygen, hemoglobin gives blood its red color.

There are far fewer white blood cells floating around in plasma. Nevertheless, these fighter cells play an equally important role in the body. White blood cells protect your body from

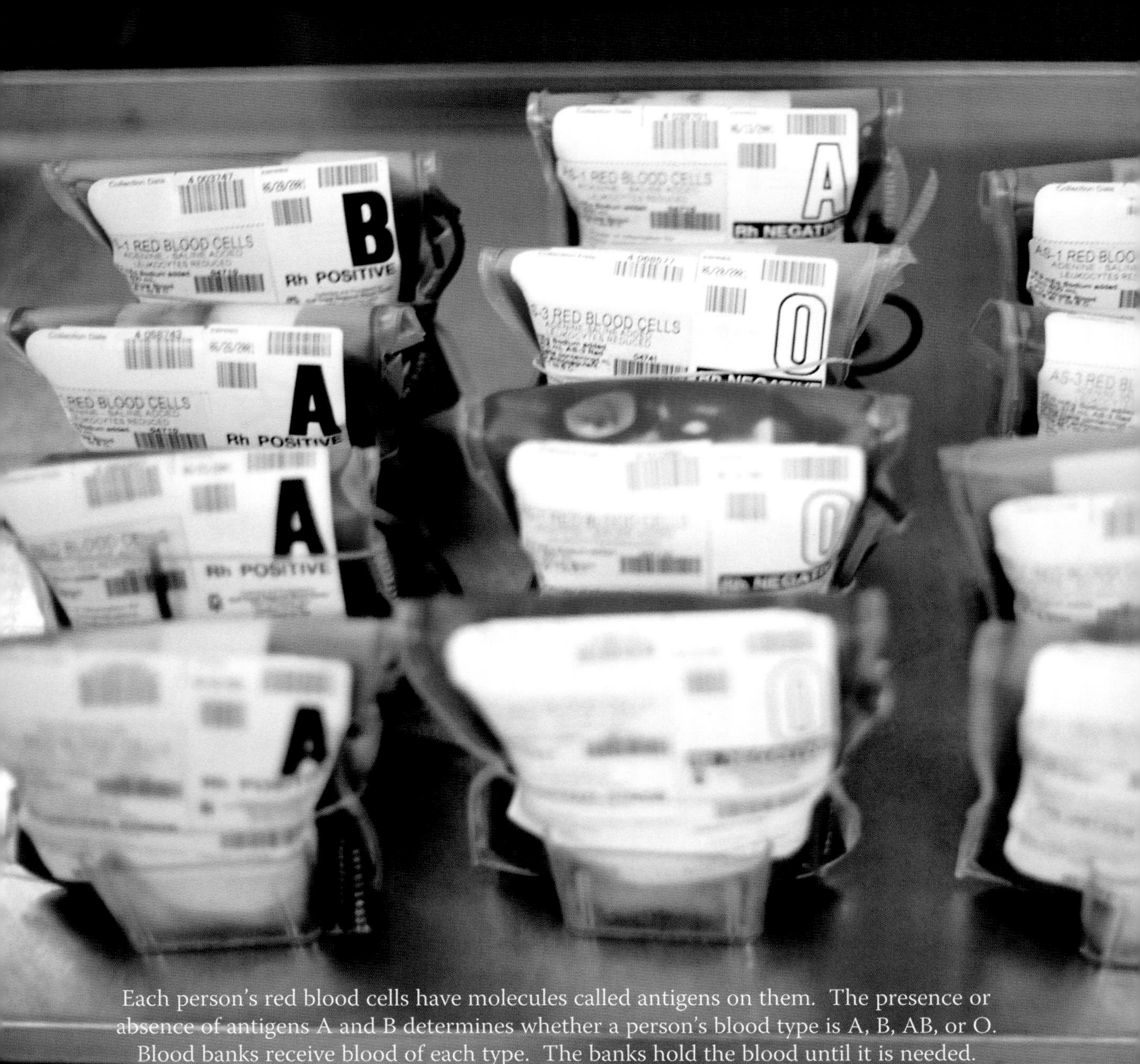

Each person's red blood cells have molecules called antigens on them. The presence or absence of antigens A and B determines whether a person's blood type is A, B, AB, or O. Blood banks receive blood of each type. The banks hold the blood until it is needed.

When you get a scrape or a cut, clean the wound with cool water. To stop bleeding, apply pressure with a cloth. If a scab forms, don't pick it off. It will fall off when it is supposed to.

invaders. When white blood cells detect unwanted **germs**, they attack and destroy them.

Some types of white blood cells can also tell the body to produce **antibodies**. After an **infection** has passed, white blood cells remember the invader. This way, they can quickly attack if the infection enters the body again.

Platelets are a child's best friend. At the site of an injury, they band together with proteins called clotting factors. In time, the platelets harden into a scab. Think twice about picking your next scab! Your platelets worked hard to put it together.

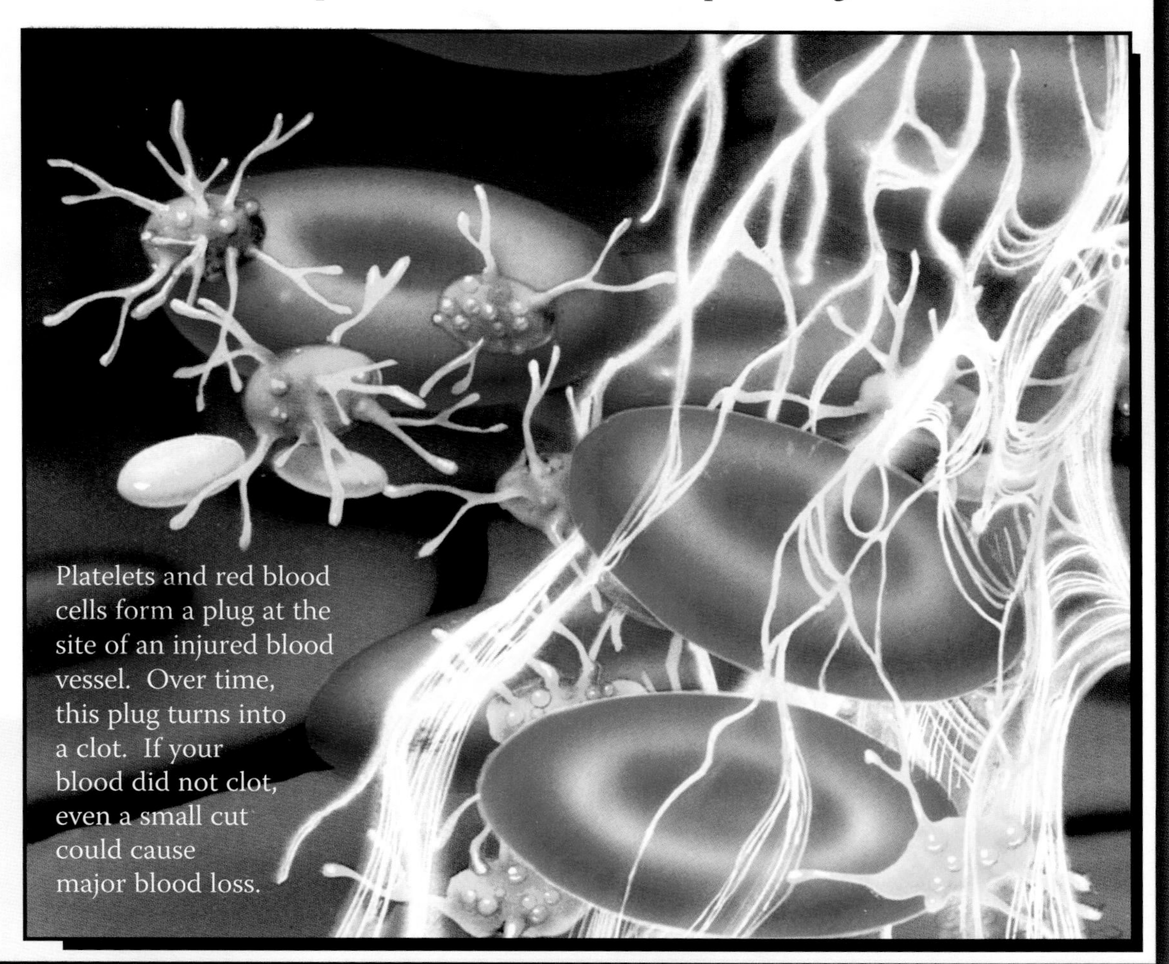

Platelets and red blood cells form a plug at the site of an injured blood vessel. Over time, this plug turns into a clot. If your blood did not clot, even a small cut could cause major blood loss.

Blood Vessels

As you know, blood doesn't just float freely under your skin. A network of blood vessels keeps it traveling to and from the right places. There are three kinds of blood vessels.

Arteries are the biggest and strongest kind of blood vessel. They supply blood to the body. Arteries take blood from the heart to the lungs. There, the blood picks up oxygen. Then, the arteries transport the oxygen-rich blood to different parts of your body. The aorta is the body's largest artery. It is attached to the heart and branches off into many smaller arteries.

Veins are the second type of blood vessel. Veins don't need to be as strong as arteries. This is because they deal with lower blood pressure. Veins carry blood after it has dropped off its cargo of oxygen. This oxygen-poor blood flows back to the heart.

The third type of blood vessel connects small arteries and veins. These tiny vessels are called capillaries. Ten capillaries equal the thickness of a human hair. Capillaries deliver blood to all **tissue** cells. Their penetrable walls allow **nutrients**, oxygen, and waste to seep in and out of your blood to your cells.

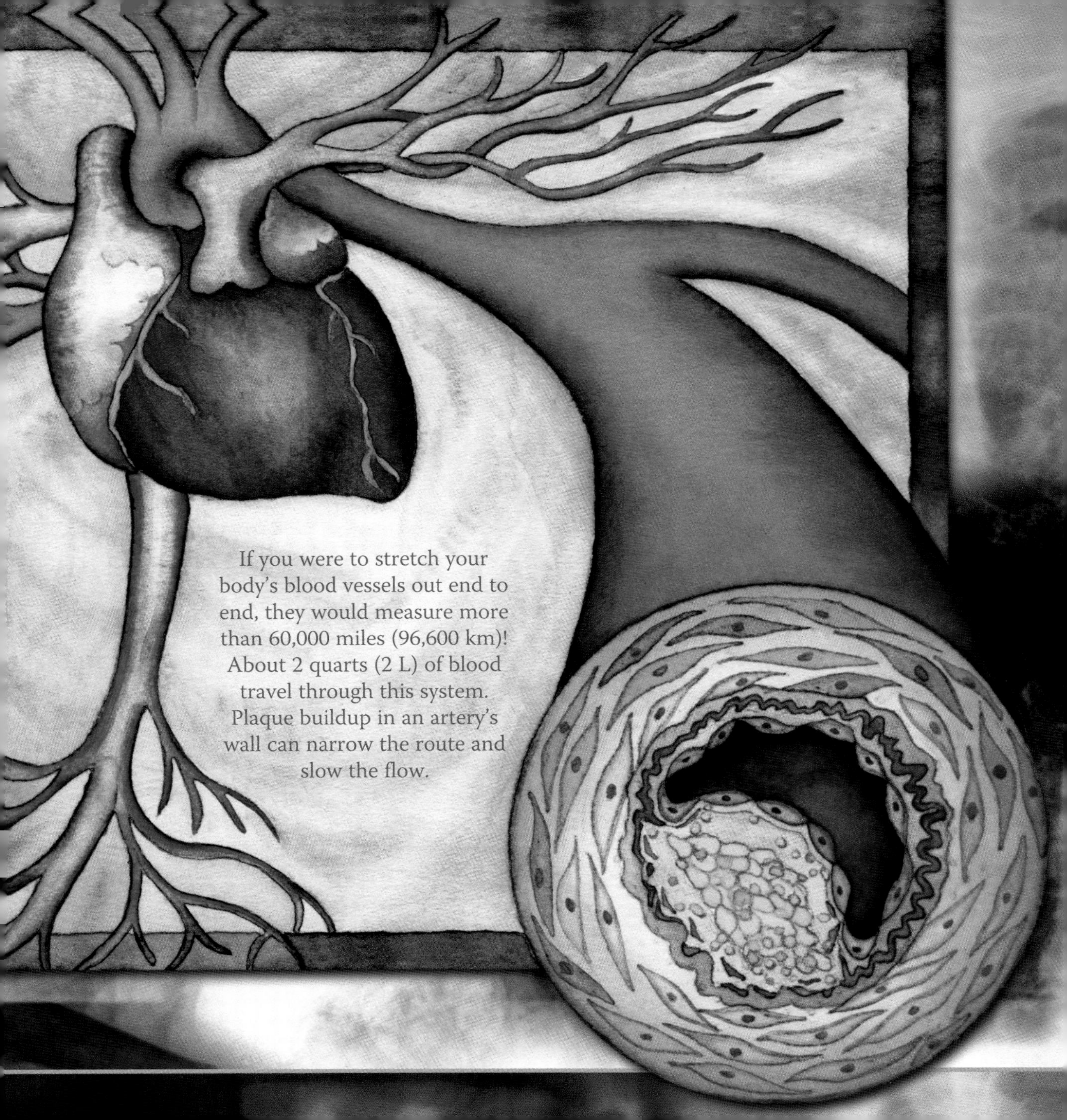

If you were to stretch your body's blood vessels out end to end, they would measure more than 60,000 miles (96,600 km)! About 2 quarts (2 L) of blood travel through this system. Plaque buildup in an artery's wall can narrow the route and slow the flow.

Pit Stop at the Cells

Stuff seeps out of your blood? Don't worry! Your body knows what it's doing. Every cell in your body needs oxygen. Capillaries allow oxygen to seep out of your blood to where it's needed.

Nutrients also seep through your capillary walls. Nutrients come from food. Your body **digests** your food into tiny particles. Then, your blood carries these particles around your body.

For example, carbohydrates from your breakfast cereal travel through your circulatory system. Carbohydrates are important sources of energy. Your cells use them as fuel. They help you think clearly in the morning.

Capillaries are the smallest blood vessels. The flow of venous blood starts in the capillaries and moves to the heart.

Start your day out right by eating a healthy breakfast!

All that work produces waste products, too. Cars burn gas and release exhaust. In a similar way, your cells burn oxygen and produce carbon dioxide. **Nutrients** also produce their own waste.

The Return Trip

The body's waste production is another normal process. Your blood picks up the garbage. But it doesn't stop there. Your blood disposes of the waste, too!

First, the carbon dioxide and other waste moves into the capillaries. Your blood moves the waste along. The capillaries join to form larger vessels called venules. Venules gradually turn into even larger vessels, your veins.

Eventually, your blood reaches two main veins. The inferior vena cava collects blood from your lower body. The superior vena cava collects blood from your head and upper body. Both of these veins then carry the blood they picked up to the heart.

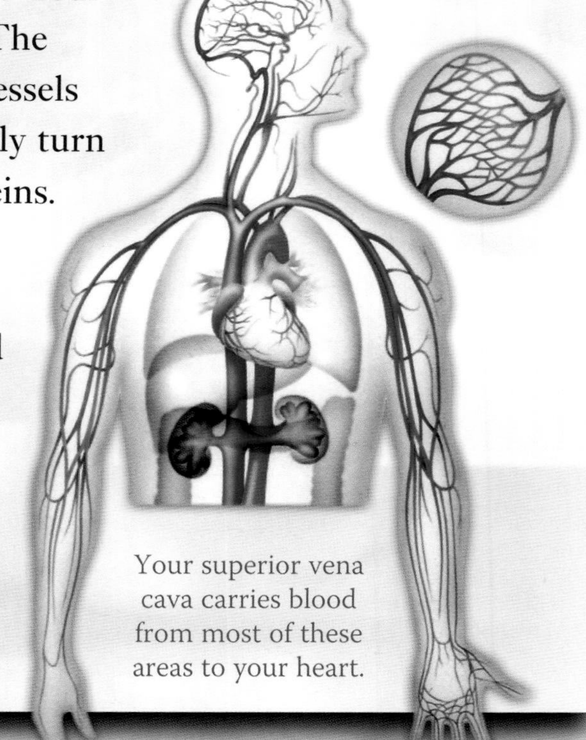

Your superior vena cava carries blood from most of these areas to your heart.

One of your chores may be to take out the garbage. Your blood takes out the garbage, too! It picks up the waste and delivers it to the proper location.

The Lungs and the Kidneys

The two venae cavae deliver blood back to your heart. Both of these large veins enter the right atrium. When the right atrium is full, your heart contracts. This contraction pushes your blood into the right ventricle. When the right ventricle is full, the heart contracts again.

From here, it's a quick trip down the **pulmonary** artery to your lungs. Soon, your blood enters the pulmonary capillaries. These special capillaries wrap around tiny air sacs called alveoli. Alveoli are full of fresh oxygen. Oxygen seeps into your blood as it passes through the capillaries.

At the same time, carbon dioxide moves out of the blood and into the air sacs. What a perfect exchange! When you exhale, your lungs release the carbon dioxide. Meanwhile, the new oxygen begins its journey to your cells.

But what about those other waste products? Your blood has to make another stop to take care of these. But first, your blood must travel back to the heart. More pumping is needed to get your blood to another destination, your kidneys.

Your kidneys filter other waste products from your blood. In fact, they filter more than 400 gallons (1,500 L) of blood per day! From the kidneys, waste leaves your body as urine. And, the filtered blood goes back to the heart.

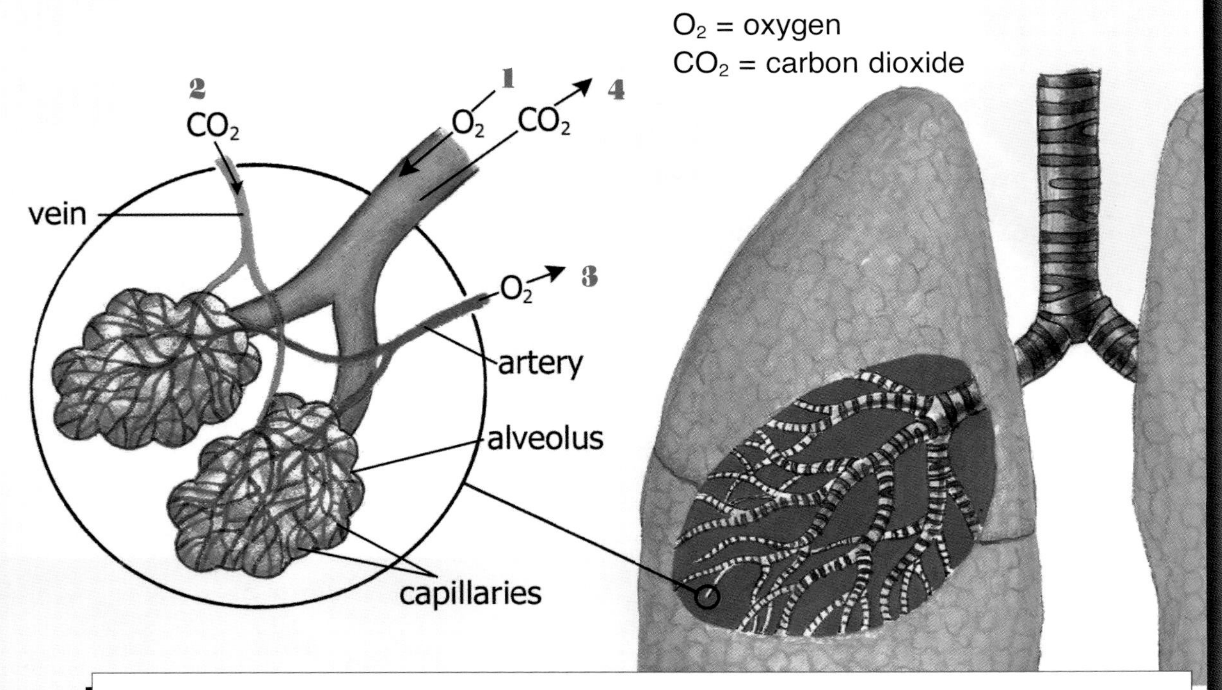

1. Oxygen enters the lungs during inhalation and reaches the alveoli.
2. Oxygen-poor blood travels through the veins into the capillaries.
3. The arteries pick up the oxygen-rich blood from the capillaries and take it to the heart.
4. Carbon dioxide leaves the body when you exhale.

A Trip Around the Body

That's a lot of information. To help sort it all out, let's follow a drop of blood through your entire circulatory system. We'll name this drop of blood Billy.

Billy starts his journey in the left atrium of your heart. Your heart contracts, and Billy rushes into the left ventricle. The mitral **valve** closes so Billy continues in the right direction. Another big contraction and Billy is forced into the aorta.

The aorta soon divides, with arteries going in many directions. For this example, we'll follow Billy to your feet. Billy moves along at a fast pace through your arteries. The arteries keep branching off. They get smaller and smaller, eventually becoming arterioles. In your toes, Billy enters your capillaries.

Once there, Billy releases the **nutrients** and oxygen he's been carrying. Your feet get happy with their new supply of energy. You can continue walking, dancing, or swimming. Now Billy

Just like you do when you are swimming, each blood cell floats in liquid. This liquid is called plasma, and it helps the blood move around the body quickly.

needs to head back to the heart. He is carrying waste and needs more oxygen.

Billy continues on this journey through the **venous** capillaries. These capillaries turn into venules and veins. Billy is returning from your lower body. Therefore, he enters your heart from the inferior vena cava.

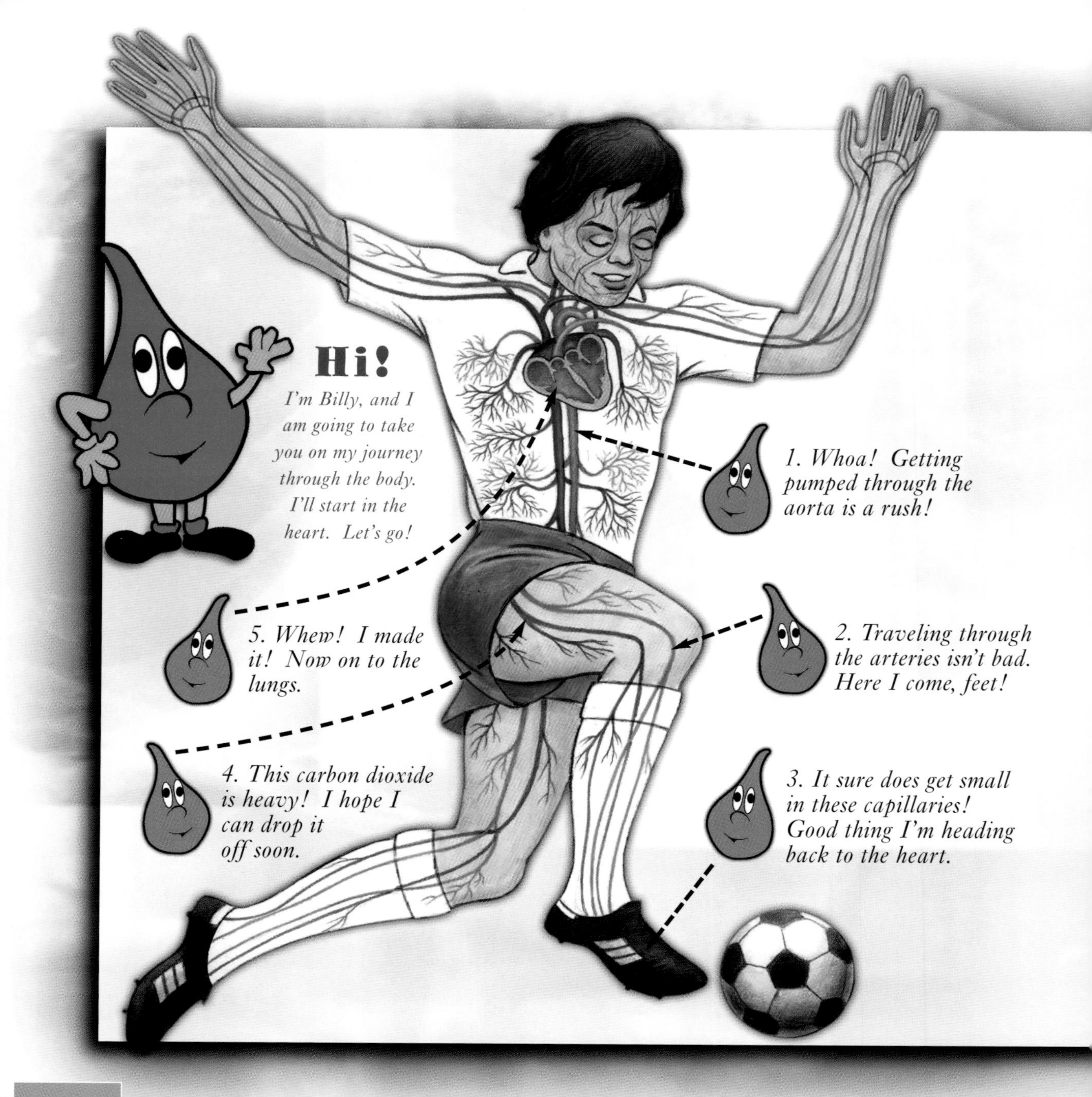
Hi!
I'm Billy, and I am going to take you on my journey through the body. I'll start in the heart. Let's go!
1. Whoa! Getting pumped through the aorta is a rush!
2. Traveling through the arteries isn't bad. Here I come, feet!
3. It sure does get small in these capillaries! Good thing I'm heading back to the heart.
4. This carbon dioxide is heavy! I hope I can drop it off soon.
5. Whew! I made it! Now on to the lungs.

After a short stop in the right atrium, Billy moves into the right ventricle. When your heart contracts, Billy is pushed out of the heart again. This time, he travels through the **pulmonary** artery to the lungs. There, Billy collects oxygen and releases carbon dioxide in the alveoli. Billy returns to the heart through a pulmonary vein, and he is back to his starting point.

Amazingly, Billy made his way through this whole cycle in about one minute! Some things affect how easily blood makes its way around the circulatory system. Blood pressure is one of these factors. Blood pressure is the force your blood puts against your vessels as it rushes through them.

The rate at which your heart contracts also affects circulation. Your heart beats faster and slower with different activities. Exercising requires more oxygen and fuel, so your heart pumps faster. Sleeping needs less, so your heart slows while you snooze.

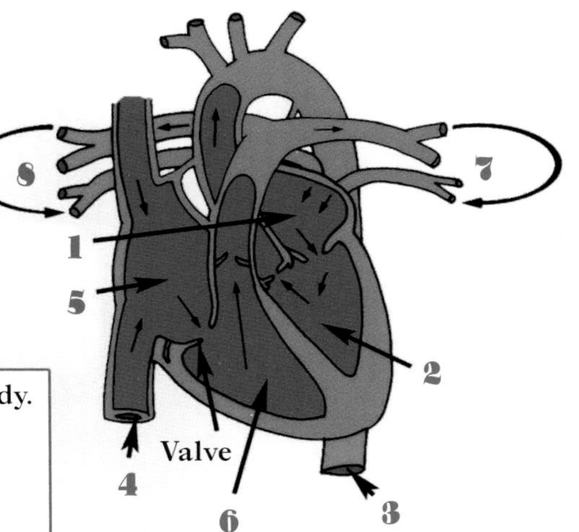

Billy started at #1 and was pumped into the body.
He returned at #4 and went on to the lungs.

1. Left Atrium
2. Left Ventricle
3. Aorta
4. Inferior Vena Cava
5. Right Atrium
6. Right Ventricle
7. Left Lung
8. Right Lung

Diseases

By now you can appreciate the hard work of your circulatory system. Your heart, blood vessels, lungs, and kidneys are pretty amazing. Unfortunately, it is not a sure thing that these **organs** will always work correctly.

Sometimes people are born with heart and circulatory problems. These are called congenital **disorders**. For example, some people are born with a heart murmur. A heart murmur is an unusual sound heard when listening to a heartbeat. In this condition, blood may flow backward through faulty **valves**. Many people live well with this condition throughout their lives. But, some people need to have it repaired.

The second type of heart and circulatory problem is acquired. This means that

Atherosclerosis is a thickening and hardening of arteries. This often affects blood flow in the coronary arteries. And, it is a primary cause of heart attacks.

the problem develops as a person ages. Coronary artery disease is the most common heart **disorder** in adults. With this disease, blood vessels harden or get clogged. Blood flow slows, or even stops if there is a clot. This can lead to a heart attack.

Hypertension, or high blood pressure, is another dangerous disorder. Over time, too much pressure can cause damage to the heart, arteries, and other **organs**. Even infants, children, and teenagers can have high blood pressure. This may be from **genetic** factors, poor diet, or lack of exercise.

About 8 in 1,000 babies have a congenital heart disease. A heart murmur may be the first sign of a defect.

Healthy Upkeep

It is important to keep your circulatory system in top form. If you start now, it will be easy! You should exercise, eat a healthy diet, and stay away from harmful substances.

Exercise helps strengthen your muscles, including your heart muscle. Fun activities such as running, dancing, and biking make your heart beat faster. This is the heart's form of exercise and will make it stronger.

A wholesome diet provides your body with energy. Make sure you eat a variety of foods to get different vitamins and minerals. Your body needs these to be strong. Remember to eat foods from all of the food groups, and limit junk food.

Last, treat your body right. Don't smoke cigarettes or take drugs. These things are terrible for your circulatory system. Too much stress isn't good for you either. So, smile a lot and be thankful for your circulatory system.

Opposite page: Want to know another way to stay healthy? Go to your doctor for regular medical checkups.

Glossary

antibody - protein produced by the body to fight off germs and other bacteria.

digest - to break down food into substances small enough for the body to absorb.

disorder - a physical or mental illness.

genetic - of or relating to the branch of biology that deals with the principles of heredity.

germ - a tiny living organism, especially one that causes disease.

infection - a disease or other harmful condition resulting from germs invading the body.

nutrient - a substance found in food and used in the body to promote growth, maintenance, and repair.

organ - a part of an animal or a plant that is composed of several kinds of tissues and that performs a specific function. The heart, liver, gallbladder, and intestines are organs of an animal.

pulmonary - relating to the lungs.

tissue - a group or cluster of similar cells that work together, such as a muscle.

valve - a movable part that temporarily closes a passageway or allows fluid to flow in one direction only.

venous - having blood that carries carbon dioxide. This blood gave oxygen to the tissues and received carbon dioxide waste.

Saying It

carbohydrate - kahr-boh-HEYE-drayt

hemoglobin - HEE-muh-gloh-buhn

mitral - MEYE-truhl

pulmonary - PUL-muh-nehr-ee

systemic - sihs-TEH-mihk

tricuspid - treye-KUHS-puhd

vena cava - VEE-nuh KAY-vuh

venous - VEE-nuhs

Web Sites

To learn more about the circulatory system, visit ABDO Publishing Company on the World Wide Web at **www.abdopub.com**. Web sites about the human body are featured on our Book Links page. These links are routinely monitored and updated to provide the most current information available.

INDEX

A
alveoli 20, 25
arteries 14, 20, 22, 25, 27
atria 6, 8, 20, 22, 25

B
blood pressure 14, 25, 27

C
capillaries 14, 16, 18, 20, 22, 23
carbon dioxide 4, 10, 14, 17, 18, 20, 23, 25
coronary artery disease 27

D
diet 27, 28

E
exercise 25, 27, 28

H
heart attack 27
heart murmur 26
hemoglobin 10

K
kidneys 21, 26

L
lungs 4, 6, 9, 10, 14, 20, 25, 26

M
muscles 6, 28

N
nutrients 4, 10, 14, 16, 17, 22, 28

O
oxygen 4, 10, 14, 16, 17, 20, 22, 23, 25

P
plasma 10
platelets 10, 12, 13

R
red blood cells 10

S
sternum 6

T
tissue 9, 10, 14

V
valves 8, 22, 26
veins 14, 18, 20, 23, 25
ventricles 6, 8, 9, 20, 22, 25

W
white blood cells 10, 12